Masala Dosa & Xenophobia

Jamil Shamji

Masala Dosa & Xenophobia © 2022 Jamil Shamji

All rights reserved.

No part of this publication may be reproduced, stored in a retrieval system, or transmitted, in any form or by any means, electronic, mechanical, photocopying, recording or otherwise, without the prior written permission of the presenters.

Jamil Shamji asserts the moral right to be identified as author of this work.

Presentation by *BookLeaf Publishing*

Web: www.bookleafpub.com

E-mail: info@bookleafpub.com

ISBN: 978-93-5744-956-4

First edition 2022

DEDICATION

Dedicated to my protector, my teacher, my older brother! I have suffered. I have learned. I Have Changed!

Always & Forever! 91

ACKNOWLEDGEMENT

Special shoutout to the team at *VIBE CREATIVE LABS*, without them these collections of poems would never have lived through the initial thought process!

PREFACE

Poetic Problems of Tomorrow's Brown Man

Just Another One of Those Guys

How can I convey my uniqueness?
While carrying the shadow of a billion strong
Congruence in my curry brethren
Belonging to none and yet blurred among all
Painted with the same brush
Despite the brilliance of colour and spice
I am seen as one of yet another in a long line of
Patels
Oh well
You don't define my uniqueness
I shall instead

Relinquishing the Freedom

Life breathed upon prewritten pages
Memories imbued with artificial amazement
Existing without choice
On a spinning coaxial wheel
Spiraling into a singular point of false autonomy
I have no say in where I may choose
To bend and sway in my spirit's breeze
Instead
Put to bed the naïve dreams
Baba I know I mustn't disappoint
But let me breathe in all that is me

The Family Fear

Love for God learned through fear
Love for parents learned through fear
Love for siblings learned through fear
Love for society learned through fear
Love for trauma learned through fear
Love for failure learned through fear
Love for fear
Learned through fear
If only I wasn't afraid to love myself

We Know You Can Do Much Better

There's little patience
Given to those unwilling to become doctors
Of their own self destruction
God help those passionate about construction
Exchanging family shame for a skilled trade
Dealing in Desi doomsday demands
Please pray for the engineers too afraid to hack
their own DNA
Thousands of dollars spent to holler and twitch
In a cookie cutter mold not built for you
The spice route spun into a silicone valley
Siphoning the ancient soul from people of the
earth
Spoiled by connectivity to the cloudiest of skies
How can archaic expectations compete?
With day-trading, single-malt whiskeys
And exotic thighs with a side of fries
The American dream versus the image of me
Death by exposure to external influence
Living in the image of every brown kid in my
life

Matha Mundu Madness

The myth of mental health
Is that it matters
Given that the only spice they want in life
Is pinches of masala on a plate
Please don't rock the boat
When the one they came in was smooth enough
Amid the torrid waves of a new day
How dare you remain in pain
When their blood
Sweat
And tears were meant to bring you clear skies
How dare you fixate on thoughts born from hate
And compulsions needing immediate action
prescribed
Too taboo to be named anything other than
Jadoo
The djinn is the daily denial
Systemic in Shaitan's nature
Skeleton's in the closet
Forbidden spirits in my head

Hey What Ever Happened To…

The ingenious design of our mind circles around
its imminently
Ticking time-bomb turnabout
Where man can flip on a binary and finally
disobey
The super ego
Crack the egg of reason
And spill the yolk of untold truths over the ears
of those that don't care
The rantings and ravings may fall on deaf ears
But the words are better spit out than internally
heard
Getting it all out
Until they are told to get out themselves

Words

Obligation
Frustration
Provocation
Indoctrination
Condemnation
Commodification
Personification
Rationalization
A whole lotta love for natively cultural rules
While not even being born in that nation

The Prewritten Verse

Dominoes fall but they fall together
A cosmic togetherness bound by prophetic plans
Taught from young ages that our lives are
written in the stars
Shining only as bright as ancestral dreams
Archaic in nature and yet tortuously prevalent
today
Dad determines job
Dad determines career
Mom manages wife
Mom monopolizes love
Their passing of the torch is a flame we may
never have asked to hold
What else is there to do but continue the chain?
A page in my family's legacy but the words
doesn't change, only the names

Get Out

Fresh off the boat
Just jumped the border
Late landing off the plane
What other euphemisms
Do youth listen to in classrooms too colourful to
think blandly?
The outsider knows they are the outsider
Once labelled and listed on the inside
A hundred different sayings and slang
To say you don't belong
And yet not a single word or phrase
To reframe the idea that differences might be
cool

Dictatorship

Have we escaped tyranny
And turmoil
Or brought the political onslaught
Simply into the living room
Hidden from the outside vibe
Eastern promises still burn hot in the West
A test of moral fibre failed by bringing the
oppression
To a new home
For now, we are left no longer praying for a
safer land
But a more understanding home

The Kohinoor Diamond

Baba can't bare to bless his jalebi baby with a co
sign for Karan to carry her away
His prized possession that was never his to
possess is now another man's to unrightfully
claim
How can he slow down the maturation of this
mehndi queen?
How can he make her love rolling Atta in her
own home?
Alone and quiet is how he loves her best
His own caged songbird
For no other gunda to hear
The prized jewel
Daughters in chains

Damn the Borders, We Look the Same

My brain is a hot moong dal soup
Liquefied by the lies and secret truths
That hide the true roots of my heritage and such
Beyond the bus stop monologues about identity
and ideas
I'm unclear on my position blessed with such
royal ancient blood
For when I see first-hand the third-world
struggle
Ghosts of feelings passed bubble to the surface
rocking my paradigm to the ground
I am no more an individual than an old tree
Housing eons of existence upon each branch
And yet with each chance given
I try to fly away
Denying the strength of well-grounded roots
An identity crisis of epic proportions
Extorting post-colonial prejudice for all that its
worth
How sad that to be identified by someone else's
divisions
A partition of logic to say the least

Praise to the Most High

The brutal irony
Of a God-fearing culture
Is that God never required fear for submission
Rather intuition would suggest that
Obligations of galactic proportions
Are far more concerning
Than late-night prayers for an A+ in Math
Does our fast appease the Almighty?
Do five prayers channel the Creator more than
just three?
Do my dietary choices determine the divine
dividend of my death?
Does He even care to be named with a capital
letter?
Unfettered thoughts may not be halal if not first
framed as humour
But humour this, how shall we fear the very
hammer we swing on others in judgement?
And perhaps the all seeing eye in the sky
Pedals the wheels of karma
Out of nothing but pure fun

How hilarious would salutations to the sun
suddenly be
When natural disasters are like the long distance
calls
From father up above

My Mother Has Been on the Phone & There's a Story to Tell

Droplets of defamation ripple brilliantly through
the waves of emotions
When shame and dignity are commodities traded
daily in caste and creed
Among other arbitrarily ass-minded divisions
Rumours are ribbons to the ugly present of past
insecurities
Now fuelling the poisonous minds of future
generations
Engineered to perform cheap soap opera drama
Politicking time away
Too naïve to see that spurned chachas and
chachis
Want nothing better than to wind up the new
generation
With the beef's and bullshit of the past
Let that pettiness go!

The Great White Stare

Fully cool in Bollywood flair
The kulfi melts in the Eurocentric eye
Kajal lines hide true darkness within
Scared to engage in colonial sin
Exoticism serves as the schism
Between decency and disrespect
To titillate the fetishist tikka tastes
Fantasies of seasoned lives
For those living stale and dry
Uncooked rice.

Sari (Sorry)

Internalized shame
In the sheen and shine of salwars and saris alike
How brutally sad
The irony is
That youth hide in embarrassment
Fearing harassment in being woefully
misunderstood
For wearing the colours, silks and dyes
Their parents never could
Weekends at temple
Fridays at mosque
Connections with God severed by
Several negative thoughts
Disregarding a rich history of textile
For texted trends on style
Sad little child
Don't feel afraid to walk through the mall
In the clothes your mother dreamed to create a
family with.

The Heat From The East

How I sorely miss
The heat from the east
Bursting through airplane doors
Floored by the arduous journey through the
clouds
A noise of smells married by honks
Beeps, and feet moving in schools of what looks
like thousands
A lifetime in reach for pennies on the dollar
Deeper look into so-called lives of squalor
The masterpiece is the hot resilience of ancient
kingdoms once strong
For the third world
Is the first reality
And the ground zero site for innovation
Thus many are growing old
With the cold indoctrination
Of festering sunburn from the gaze of westerner
bums
Not ready to enjoy the historic heat from the east
Stop sweating it's just words.

Yo…Gah, yuck!

Zen for sale
Lotus imagery,
Or was it a sun?
Who knows when appropriation is this fun
Inhale, stretch and exhale
Capitalist troubles breathed away upon mystic
truths
Polymer mats match the flattened spirit of sage
elders
Turning in their graves
Knowing bimbos and buffoons bust moves
Of vulgar hilarity
Flaring and flinging in the name of the most
spiritual
Rituals and rites tightly wound around
Chakras and choices to live slightly more purely
For the action is a lifestyle
And a culture untold
Yoga.

Submission of Goodness

One cannot recognize the warmth of care
If they have only been taught it to be an action to
expect
Or a duty to provide
Feelings reside in dusty canals of the heart
Rarely touched
Can one even long for that which they've
Truly never felt
Colonized learning consolidated through
positive and negative reinforcement
Smile
Be pleasant
And shine their shoes... metaphorically of course
Kiss the ring so to say
Married to the pain of a careful life without care.

In Between

Melanated magic
From Caucasus roots
The bhoot of my past
Creates horrors for the future
In my mind
Marketed as "or else" thinking
Blinking back the tears of being denied
The opportunity to fit in
To the light and dark dichotomy
Contradictions galore
Making brown out of the grey
Find me in the gaps.

See You Soon…But Just Not Yet

Days do not turn to nights
Without witnessing a fight between angels and
demons
Waging war on the reason to survive with guilt
Sword at the hilt
We are no longer at odds
And yet the urge to get even will never be
addressed
I confess
I'm for once not too sure of what to do
Vivid memories fade like sand falling through
hands
While these clenched fists seem impossible to
open
Hoping pathetically
That you were on an island with rappers
unnamed
Faking your death to bring magnitude
To the already magnificent legacy you've
displayed
I should know
The caretaker of your shadow

Dusting away the cobwebs of friends shedding
tears at your bed
They said
We said
I said
It wasn't real
And yet there you've gone
And we're still here
How longingly I fondly gaze up at the stars
To join you in this intergalactic trance
And dance through existence with such debonair
flair
My life test is to finesse day-to-day displeasure
with my state of being
Fleeing opportunities to embrace the right to live
For the wrong in joy
Is as loud as ever
Perhaps I am treasuring the opportunity to be
punished
Weathering the futility of old thoughts
perennially rummaged
For new breakthroughs
New insights
On old wounds that won't heal
The zeal to zig-zag through adulthood is no
longer that zesty
God you may no longer impress me with the
miracles of fickle faith

I believed and given the opportunity to leave,
still stayed strong in the head
Impatient in my exhaustion, reverse the
language and from up, I will be fed
I hope to see you soon…but for our mother just
not yet
91.